THURGOOD **MARSHALL**

and Equal Rights

by Seamus Cavan

GATEWAY CIVIL RIGHTS
THE MILLBROOK PRESS
BROOKFIELD, CONNECTICUT

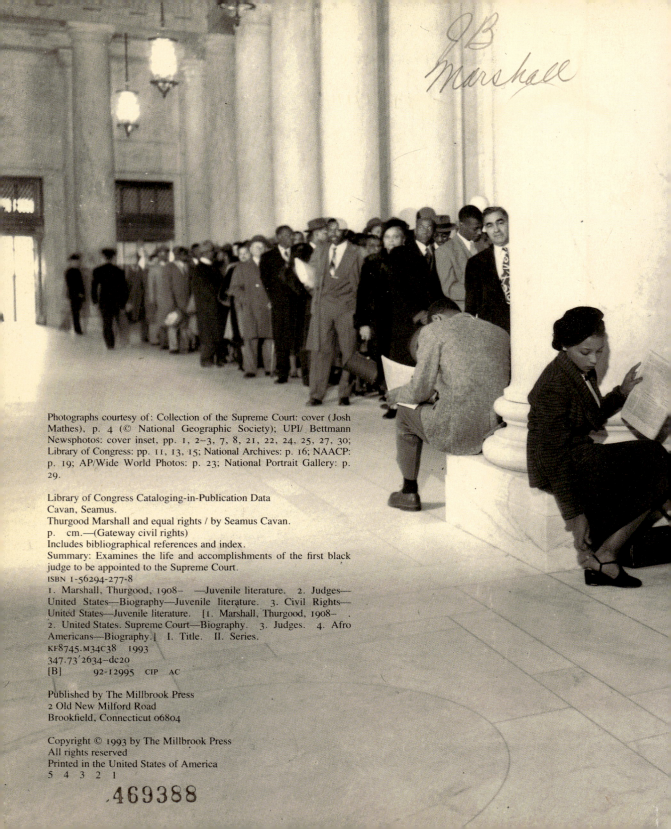

JB
Marshall

Photographs courtesy of: Collection of the Supreme Court: cover (Josh Mathes), p. 4 (© National Geographic Society); UPI/ Bettmann Newsphotos: cover inset, pp. 1, 2–3, 7, 8, 21, 22, 24, 25, 27, 30; Library of Congress: pp. 11, 13, 15; National Archives: p. 16; NAACP: p. 19; AP/Wide World Photos: p. 23; National Portrait Gallery: p. 29.

Library of Congress Cataloging-in-Publication Data
Cavan, Seamus.
Thurgood Marshall and equal rights / by Seamus Cavan.
p.   cm.—(Gateway civil rights)
Includes bibliographical references and index.
Summary: Examines the life and accomplishments of the first black judge to be appointed to the Supreme Court.
ISBN 1-56294-277-8
1. Marshall, Thurgood, 1908– —Juvenile literature. 2. Judges—United States—Biography—Juvenile literature. 3. Civil Rights—United States—Juvenile literature. [1. Marshall, Thurgood, 1908– . 2. United States. Supreme Court—Biography. 3. Judges. 4. Afro Americans—Biography.] I. Title. II. Series.
KF8745.M34C38 1993
347.73′2634—dc20
[B]   92-12995 CIP AC

Published by The Millbrook Press
2 Old New Milford Road
Brookfield, Connecticut 06804

469388

1952 segregation hearings at the U.S. Supreme Court, Washington, D.C.

Like many young boys, Thurgood Marshall often got into mischief. He was never a serious troublemaker, but he liked to have fun, and he didn't always do exactly what his parents told him to do.

Years later, Marshall remembered those early days. "We lived on a respectable street, but behind us there were back alleys where roughnecks and the tough kids hung out. When it was time for dinner, my mother used to go to the front door and call my older brother. Then she'd go to the *back* door and call me."

Thurgood caused a little trouble in school, too. He was smart, but he liked talking with his friends more than listening to the teacher.

Sometimes Thurgood's teachers just could not keep him quiet. On those days, he was sent to sit by himself on a chair in the school's basement.

It was boring in the basement. There was nothing there but some old, broken desks, some leaky pipes, a pile of coal, and the noisy boiler that heated the school. Even class was more fun than sitting alone down there. But the principal of the school had a rule. No student could return to class until he or she had read part of the United States Constitution and understood it well enough to explain it to him.

Even though he was a fun-loving boy, Thurgood Marshall had a serious, thoughtful side, too. When the principal gave him the Constitution to read, Thurgood thought of it as a chance to learn. By the time he left school, he knew the entire Constitution by heart.

But as he studied this document, Thurgood was puzzled. Over and over again, he read the words of the Fourteenth Amendment, which promises that all American citizens have equal rights under the law. He had no trouble understanding what the words meant, but when he thought about what life was like in his hometown, he knew that black Americans did not in fact have equal rights.

Thurgood Marshall was born on July 2, 1908, in West Baltimore, Maryland. When he was growing up in the early part of the twentieth century, segregation—the separation of different races of people—was common throughout the United States. In many places, it was the law of the land.

Even the lessons Thurgood learned about the meaning of the Constitution took place in the basement of an all-black school. White children went to another, better, school in the white part of town.

In other parts of the United States, blacks were not allowed to buy houses in white neighborhoods. They had to ride in separate railroad cars or at the backs of buses, while whites

THE CONSTITUTION

The Constitution is the supreme law of the United States. It was written in 1787, not long after the thirteen colonies won their freedom from England. The Constitution tells how the United States is to be governed. It also promises American citizens certain civil rights. For example, Americans are free to say what they think about their government. They can belong to whatever religion they want, and they are free to elect the leaders they want. These are called the rights to freedom of speech and freedom of religion, and the right to vote.

The amendments—changes or additions to the Constitution—give Americans certain rights that were not included when the original document was written. The Fourteenth Amendment was added in 1868, a few years after slavery was ended by the Civil War. It promised that all Americans, white or black, would receive equal rights under the law.

rode up front. They could not eat at the same restaurants as white people, or sit in the same sections at movie theaters or ballparks. Blacks had to drink from water fountains marked COLORED, while whites drank from fountains marked WHITE. Blacks were often even kept from voting.

A Florida movie house in the 1930s directs black people to a separate rear entrance.

Thurgood Marshall could not understand how segregation could exist when the Constitution promised *everyone* equal rights. He went home from school one day and asked his father, Will Marshall, how this could be. The Constitution is the way things ought to be, not the way they are, Will Marshall told his son. This answer made young Thurgood very sad and angry. He decided that when he grew up he was going to change things.

And he did just that. Thurgood Marshall became a very influential lawyer and then a Supreme Court Justice. He dedicated his life to defending the civil rights of his fellow human beings.

The Way Things Ought to Be

Thurgood Marshall never forgot the lesson his father taught him about the Constitution. While still very young, he learned another important lesson from his father, one about fighting prejudice. One day, a friend asked him what he would do if someone called him a ''nigger.'' Would he fight?

The question bothered Marshall, for he had never heard anyone use that word. He went home and asked his father what it meant. Will Marshall explained that the word was used by prejudiced, ignorant white people to insult blacks. He told his son that if anyone ever called him that name, "you not only got my permission to fight him—you got my orders to fight him." The point Will Marshall was trying to make was not that it was good to fight, but that there were some things that were worth fighting for.

Thurgood took his father's words to heart. One day, when he was in high school, a white man on a train platform called him a "nigger." Marshall did not wait for the man to say he was sorry. Instead, he hit him.

As Thurgood got older, he learned that he couldn't always fight with his fists. It was easy to punch someone who called him a name, but other kinds of prejudice were harder to fight. For example, whom could he hit when he wasn't allowed to attend the best schools because of the color of his skin? He had to learn a better way to fight.

Again, his father helped show him the way. Will Marshall made his living as a waiter, but his great love was for the law. He read about all the important court cases, and in his spare time he went to court to watch interesting trials in person. Many times, he brought Thurgood with him. At home, he and his son would discuss what they had heard in court. Will Marshall also made sure that Thurgood read the newspaper each day. Then he would ask his son questions about the articles he had read.

*A white elementary school in South Boston, Virginia, around
1930. Below, a black elementary school in the same town.*

Thurgood's mother, Norma Marshall, was a schoolteacher. She told Thurgood again and again that education was important, and she made sure that his fooling around with his friends never interfered with his schoolwork. She wanted Thurgood to become a dentist, but all that time spent reading the Constitution and talking to his father had given him a different idea. He thought that he might like to become a lawyer instead. It seemed that a lawyer might have a good chance of making the way things *were* more like the way things *ought to be.*

In 1925, when he was seventeen years old, Thurgood graduated from high school. Because most colleges did not accept black students, Marshall enrolled in Lincoln University in Pennsylvania, the nation's oldest black college. The four years he spent there were good ones. He worked hard and learned a lot. He also fell in love with a young woman named Vivian Burey, and they got married. Most important, he decided for certain that he wanted to be a lawyer.

Because he was black, Marshall was not accepted at the University of Maryland, the first law school he chose. He wound up going to Howard University in Washington, D.C., where most of the nation's black professionals were trained. It turned out to be a very wise choice.

Howard was proud to accept a student of Marshall's ability, and Marshall was eager to prove himself. After a week of classes there, he knew that Howard was the right place for him and that the law was the right course of study. The work was hard, and the days were long. But Marshall knew that what he wanted to do was important, and that the only way to succeed was through hard work. By the end of his first year, he was the top student in his class.

Marshall's favorite teacher at Howard was a brilliant lawyer named Charles Hamilton Houston. Houston taught his students that the law was the tool that black Americans could use to end segregation and to win all the rights promised them by the Constitution. The courts were the place where blacks could win equal justice, Houston told his students. But they had to be prepared, and they had to commit themselves to excellence.

Howard University students protested the 1934 National Crime Conference because the conference leaders refused to discuss the problem of lynching.

They could not allow themselves to use the prejudice they would face as an excuse for failure.

Marshall admired Houston, and he took his teacher's words very seriously. If Houston told the class to read five cases for the next day's lesson, Marshall read ten. He knew that because he was black, he would always have to be a little bit better than the white lawyers he would face. He would have to work harder than they did.

His hard work paid off. Marshall finished law school in the spring of 1933 as the top student in his class. He was ready now to go to court. Many lawyers practice law because it is a way to make a lot of money, but Marshall had different goals. He wanted to be what Charles Houston called a "social engineer," which meant someone who used the law to change society for the better. In late 1933, Thurgood Marshall opened a small law office in east Baltimore.

Equal Justice

Thurgood Marshall was a very unusual lawyer. He used all his training and ability to help others, not to make himself rich. Most of his clients were poor blacks who could not afford to pay him much or even anything at all. They came to Marshall

In 1935, Thurgood Marshall (left) and Charles Houston (right) worked with their client, Donald Gaines Murray, on a case that would make Murray the first black admitted to the University of Maryland law school.

because they were homeless, or because they had been beaten up by policemen, or because they were too poor to pay their bills. He never said no to anyone who needed his help. Soon he was known as a "little folks' lawyer," someone to whom poor people could turn for help.

Marshall also worked with an organization called the National Association for the Advancement of Colored People (NAACP). The NAACP was the nation's most important civil rights organization. Its members were dedicated to ending segregation through peaceful means.

To speak out against segregation required a great deal of courage. For many years, blacks who had done so lost their jobs or were arrested or even killed. But Marshall was not afraid. He told his fellow blacks that it was time to claim their equal rights under the law. The NAACP had a bold plan to end segregation in the United States, and Marshall was eager to play a part.

In 1938, Marshall became the chief lawyer for the NAACP. For fourteen years, he drove hundreds of thousands of miles back and forth across the country arguing court cases against segregation. Though he never earned much money for his work, he won several important cases regarding segregation and the right of blacks to vote.

As the NAACP's chief lawyer, Marshall was well known all over the country as a man who fought hard for equal rights.

By the end of the 1940s, Marshall was known as one of the best lawyers in the country. Sometimes racists threatened to kill him if he continued his work, but to black Americans and to whites who wished to see an end to prejudice, he was a hero.

But Marshall was not satisfied. He and the NAACP decided that the most important place where segregation had to be ended was in education. They had several good reasons. Education was of great importance to the future of society. Children who were denied a fair chance to receive a quality education were denied an opportunity to better themselves and to build a better life. Marshall and the NAACP also believed that if black and white children could be educated together, side by side in the same classrooms, they would learn not to hate and fear each other, and prejudice would come to an end.

In 1953, Marshall argued a case called *Brown* v. *Board of Education of Topeka, Kansas* before the Supreme Court of the United States. The *Brown* case was about black schoolchildren in Kansas, Delaware, Virginia, South Carolina, and the District of Columbia who wanted to attend integrated public schools. An integrated school is one that children of all colors and races are free to attend. The case was one of the most important that had ever been argued in front of the Supreme Court. Everyone who was involved knew that the entire future of legal segregation in the United States was at stake.

SEPARATE BUT EQUAL

The Supreme Court ruled that segregation was legal, or constitutional, in a famous case called *Plessy* v. *Ferguson*. Homer Plessy was a black man who was arrested because he refused to ride in the segregated "blacks-only" car of a train in Louisiana.

Plessy brought his case before the Supreme Court in 1896. His lawyers argued that Homer Plessy and all black people were being denied their civil rights because of segregation. His lawyers pointed out that the Fourteenth Amendment of the Constitution promised all Americans equal rights under the law.

Amazingly, the Supreme Court did not agree. The Court decided that it was all right to segregate as long as both races had equal facilities. In other words, it was all right to have separate schools for black children and for white children as long as the schools were equal. It was all right to make blacks and whites sit in separate train cars if the cars were equal.

For more than fifty years, separate-but-equal was the law of the land. What Thurgood Marshall proved in the *Brown* case was that the separate schools that black children were made to attend were never really equal to the all-white schools. More importantly, he proved to the Court that segregation under any circumstances was wrong because it was harmful to both blacks and whites and because it went against the principles of the Constitution.

Marshall easily proved that the segregated schools the black children went to were not equal to the ones attended by white students. There were fewer teachers for the black students, for example. The black schools were not given money to provide busing for their students. The all-white schools received more tax money from the government, which meant that their buildings were in better shape. But Marshall did not end his argument there. If he had, those who supported segregation could have promised to improve the black schools and make them equal to the white ones. That way, black and white students would still have to attend separate schools.

*Separate-but-equal schools
existed in name only.*

Instead, Marshall tried to show the nine justices, or judges, of the Supreme Court that segregation was extremely harmful to black youngsters. He presented testimony from teachers, doctors, and other experts to prove that segregation caused black children to feel inferior and lessened their desire to learn. In this way, segregation denied black children the chance to reach their full potential. He also told the justices that the men who wrote the Fourteenth Amendment had meant for all citizens, black or white, to get equal rights under the law.

In the *Brown* case, Marshall used all the power and skills he had learned in a lifetime of hard work and dedication. The Supreme Court took five months to decide the case. On May 17, 1954, Chief Justice Earl Warren finally read the court's decision. "Education is the most important function of state and local governments," Warren said. Then he asked the question: "Does segregation of children in public schools solely on the basis of race deprive the children of the minority group of equal educational opportunities?" After a brief pause, he provided the court's answer, which an entire nation was waiting to hear.

"We believe that it does. To separate [black schoolchildren] from others solely because of their race generates a feeling of inferiority that may affect their hearts and minds in a way unlikely ever to be undone. We conclude unanimously that in the field of public education the doctrine of 'separate but equal' has no place. Separate educational facilities are inherently unequal."

NAACP lawyers George E. C. Hayes (left), Thurgood Marshall, and James M. Nabrit (right) leave the court house on May 17, 1954, after their victory in the landmark case of Brown v. Board of Education.

Little Folks' Lawyer
on the High Court

Marshall had no time to rest after his historic victory in the *Brown* case. Many Americans were not happy that he had changed the way they were used to living. In many places people tried to keep black students from going to schools that had been for white children only. In the state of Arkansas, the governor even tried to use soldiers to keep the schools from being integrated. Blacks who tried to obtain their equal rights under the law were sometimes beaten or arrested or even killed. Black churches were bombed.

Racist hecklers backed by the National Guard try to keep a black student from entering Central High School in Little Rock, Arkansas.

But men like Thurgood Marshall and his friend Dr. Martin Luther King, Jr., a famous civil rights leader, were not frightened. King and Marshall and many other Americans kept on working to make American society live up to the words of the Constitution. For Marshall, that meant more long hours working for the NAACP. He traveled around the country, standing up to threats of violence and death, to bring lawsuits against school districts that refused to obey the *Brown* decision.

In 1961, President John F. Kennedy appointed Thurgood Marshall a judge on the U.S. Court of Appeals. Marshall proved to be an excellent judge. He was especially wise on those cases that involved civil rights. The Supreme Court did not change even one of Marshall's decisions. This was a remarkable record.

An angry-looking Marshall arrives at the Little Rock District Court, where a hearing was held to demand that Arkansas Governor Orval Faubus allow integration in state schools.

His outstanding work won him more honors. In 1965, he was asked by President Lyndon Johnson to become the solicitor general, the chief lawyer of the country. Two years later, Marshall received the highest honor a lawyer can receive when Johnson asked him to be a justice of the U.S. Supreme Court.

Thurgood Marshall is sworn in as the new U.S. Solicitor General in 1965. From left to right, Marshall's children, Thurgood, Jr., and John; his wife; and President Lyndon Johnson look on.

*Thurgood Marshall was the first black Supreme Court
justice in the history of the United States.*

Marshall was the first black man to serve on the Supreme Court.
Becoming a Supreme Court justice was a great achievement for
him and for all black Americans. The president said that Marshall had already earned a place in American history.

THE SUPREME COURT

Even though the words of the Constitution are easy to read, understanding what they mean is not. Lawyers, lawmakers, and citizens often do not agree on what is the right way to understand, or interpret, the Constitution. Deciding what the Constitution means is the job of the United States Supreme Court.

The United States has been an independent country for more than two hundred years. In that time, the Constitution has been interpreted to mean many different things. For example, during the first eighty-nine years of this country's history, slavery was legal. Millions of blacks were made to live as slaves, even though the Declaration of Independence clearly says that "all men are created equal."

In 1857, in a very famous case called *Dred Scott* v. *Sandford*, the Supreme Court even ruled that blacks were not citizens of the United States.

After the Civil War, in 1865, slavery was made illegal. The Fourteenth Amendment was added to the Constitution. It promised that all Americans, white or black, would receive equal rights under the law. Even so, many states passed laws that continued to allow segregation, and the Supreme Court determined that this was legal. It took almost one hundred years and the work of many heroic people, like Thurgood Marshall, to convince the Supreme Court that segregation was unconstitutional.

The U.S. Supreme Court in 1990: (top row, left to right) Anthony Kennedy, Sandra Day O'Connor, Antonin Scalia, and David Souter; (bottom row, left to right) Harry Blackmun, Byron White, William Rehnquist, Thurgood Marshall, and John Paul Stevens.

Marshall served on the Supreme Court until 1991, when he retired. Even on the Supreme Court he remained a lawyer for the little folks, a person who fought for the rights of all Americans. He always remembered that some people did not have the help of loving parents or concerned teachers, and he tried to make sure that the law looked out for these people, too. Thurgood Marshall devoted his life to making sure that American society gave a fair chance to all its citizens. Few Americans have done as much to make their country a better place.

IMPORTANT DATES IN THE LIFE OF THURGOOD MARSHALL

1908   Thurgood Marshall is born in West Baltimore, Maryland, on July 2.

1925   Marshall begins college at Lincoln University, Pennsylvania.

1929   Marshall begins law school at Howard University, Washington, D.C.

1933   Marshall opens a law office in East Baltimore, Maryland.

1938   Marshall becomes chief lawyer for the NAACP.

1954   Marshall wins the case of *Brown* v. *Board of Education,* which makes segregation in public schools illegal.

1961   Marshall becomes a judge on the U.S. Court of Appeals.

1965   Marshall becomes the solicitor general.

1967   Marshall is appointed a justice on the U.S. Supreme Court.

1991   Thurgood Marshall retires.

FIND OUT MORE ABOUT
THURGOOD MARSHALL AND HIS TIMES

The Constitution by Warren Colman (Chicago, Ill.: Childrens Press, 1987).

I Have a Dream: The Life and Words of Martin Luther King, Jr., by Jim Haskins (Brookfield, Conn.: The Millbrook Press, 1992).

Martin Luther King, Jr. by Rita Hakim (Brookfield, Conn.: The Millbrook Press, 1991).

The Picture Life of Thurgood Marshall by Margaret B. Young (New York: Franklin Watts, 1971).

Thurgood Marshall: The Fight for Equal Justice by Debra Hess (Englewood Cliffs, N.J.: Silver Burdett Press, 1990).

Thurgood Marshall: Supreme Court Justice by Lisa Aldred (New York: Chelsea House Publishers, 1990).

Six school children from Little Rock Central High School sit with NAACP leaders Bates and Marshall on the steps of the Supreme Court in 1958.

INDEX

jB
MARSHALL

Cavan, Seamus

Thurgood Marshall and
equal rights

469388

$11.90

DISCARD

DATE			

CHECKERBOARD BIOGRAPHY LIBRARY

U.S. PRESIDENTS

The
United States Presidents

LYNDON B. JOHNSON

ABDO Publishing Company

Megan M. Gunderson

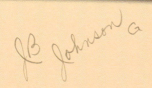

visit us at
www.abdopublishing.com

Published by ABDO Publishing Company, 8000 West 78th Street, Edina, Minnesota 55439. Copyright © 2009 by Abdo Consulting Group, Inc. International copyrights reserved in all countries. No part of this book may be reproduced in any form without written permission from the publisher. The Checkerboard Library™ is a trademark and logo of ABDO Publishing Company.

Printed in the United States.

Cover Photo: Lyndon Baines Johnson Library and Museum
Interior Photos: AP Images pp. 13, 14, 17; Corbis pp. 19, 20; iStockphoto p. 32; Lyndon Baines
    Johnson Library and Museum pp. 9, 11, 18, 21, 23, 24, 25, 26, 27, 28, 29; Lyndon Baines
    Johnson Library and Museum photo by Frank Muto p. 5

Editor: BreAnn Rumsch
Art Direction & Cover Design: Neil Klinepier
Interior Design: Neil Klinepier

Library of Congress Cataloging-in-Publication Data

Gunderson, Megan M., 1981-
  Lyndon B. Johnson / Megan M. Gunderson.
      p. cm. -- (The United States presidents)
  Includes index.
  ISBN 978-1-60453-462-7
  1. Johnson, Lyndon B. (Lyndon Baines), 1908-1973--Juvenile literature. 2. Presidents--United
States--Biography--Juvenile literature. I. Title.

  E847.G86 2009
  973.923092--dc22
  [B]
                                    2008025596

CONTENTS

LYNDON B. JOHNSON

At 2:38 PM on November 22, 1963, Lyndon B. Johnson became the thirty-sixth U.S. president. The new president took the oath of office on the presidential airplane, Air Force One. It was unlike any other **inauguration**.

Less than two hours earlier, President John F. Kennedy had been **assassinated**. He had been riding through downtown Dallas, Texas. There, he had been shot.

The entire nation was in shock over the loss of its president. Later that day, Air Force One landed at Andrews Air Force Base near Washington, D.C. There, Johnson said, "This is a sad time for all people. We have suffered a loss that cannot be weighed." He added, "I will do my best. That is all I can do. I ask for your help – and God's."

As president, Johnson carried out many of Kennedy's plans for the nation. His popularity soared. In 1964, Americans elected Johnson to a full term. He successfully started many of his

4

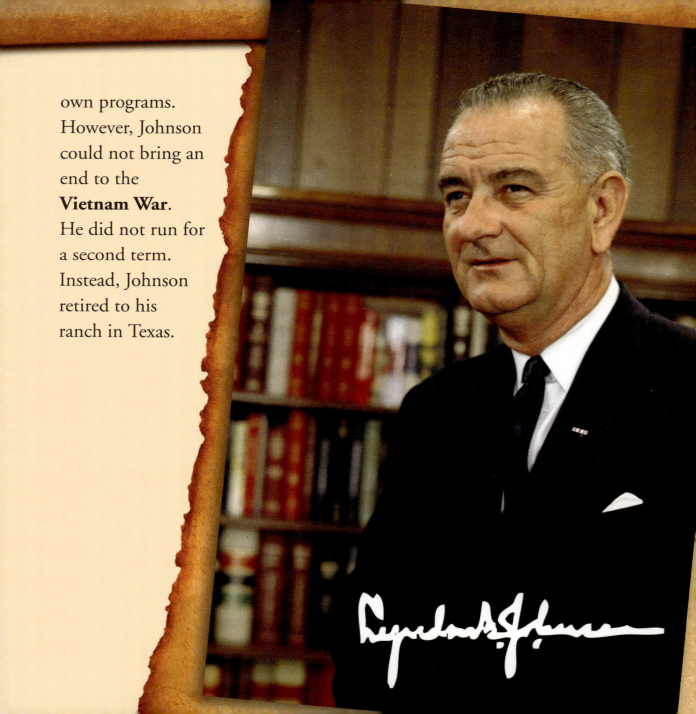

own programs. However, Johnson could not bring an end to the **Vietnam War**. He did not run for a second term. Instead, Johnson retired to his ranch in Texas.

TIMELINE

1908 - On August 27, Lyndon Baines Johnson was born near Stonewall, Texas.

1931 - Johnson moved to Washington, D.C., to work for Representative Richard M. Kleberg.

1934 - On November 17, Johnson married Claudia Alta "Lady Bird" Taylor.

1935 - Johnson became director of the National Youth Administration in Texas.

1937 - Johnson was elected to the U.S. House of Representatives.

1941 - Johnson began serving in World War II.

1944 - Johnson's daughter Lynda Bird was born.

1947 - Johnson's daughter Luci Baines was born.

1948 - Johnson was elected to the U.S. Senate.

1960 - Johnson was elected vice president under John F. Kennedy.

1963 - On November 22, President Kennedy was assassinated; Johnson became president.

1964 - On July 2, President Johnson signed the Civil Rights Act; Johnson was elected president.

1966 - Johnson appointed the first African-American head of a cabinet department, Robert C. Weaver.

1967 - Johnson appointed the first African-American Supreme Court justice, Thurgood Marshall.

1968 - On March 31, President Johnson declared he would not run for reelection.

1971 - Johnson's book *The Vantage Point: Perspectives of the Presidency, 1963–1969* was published; the Lyndon Baines Johnson Library and Museum was dedicated.

1973 - On January 22, Lyndon B. Johnson died of a heart attack.

When Lyndon B. Johnson was born, his grandfather Samuel Ealy Johnson Sr. said, "He'll be a United States senator some day."

The entire Johnson family had the same initials. *LBJ* stood for Lyndon Baines Johnson and Lady Bird Johnson. It also stood for their daughters, Lynda Bird Johnson and Luci Baines Johnson.

The Lyndon B. Johnson National Historical Park includes Johnson's birthplace and his childhood home.

The Manned Spacecraft Center in Houston, Texas, is now called the Lyndon B. Johnson Space Center. It was renamed in 1973 in honor of Johnson's support of the space program.

GROWING UP

Lyndon Baines Johnson was born on August 27, 1908, near Stonewall, Texas. He was the oldest of five children. Lyndon's parents were Samuel Ealy Johnson Jr. and Rebekah Baines Johnson. Samuel was a farmer and a schoolteacher. He also was a member of the Texas House of Representatives. Rebekah had graduated from Baylor University in Waco, Texas. She had also been a teacher before she married.

When Lyndon was five, his family moved to Johnson City, Texas. Lyndon's grandfather had been one of the town founders. Growing up, Lyndon did various jobs to help support the family. He shined shoes in the barbershop. And, he herded goats for ranchers.

In school, Lyndon was an average student. He did not like studying, but he earned good grades. Lyndon was

FAST FACTS

BORN - August 27, 1908
WIFE - Claudia Alta "Lady Bird" Taylor (1912–2007)
CHILDREN - 2
POLITICAL PARTY - Democrat
AGE AT INAUGURATION - 55
YEARS SERVED - 1963–1969
VICE PRESIDENT - Hubert H. Humphrey
DIED - January 22, 1973, age 64

8

Rebekah Baines Johnson

Samuel Ealy Johnson Jr.

better known for his leadership skills. He was class president and participated in **debate**.

In 1924, Lyndon graduated from high school. His parents wanted him to go to college, but he disagreed. Instead, Lyndon and some friends headed to California.

There, Lyndon did a variety of jobs. These included picking grapes and working as a law clerk. Yet Lyndon hardly made enough money to buy food. He returned to Johnson City and worked as a road builder. Soon, Lyndon was ready for college.

TEACHER AND HUSBAND

    In 1927, Johnson set out for Southwest Texas State Teachers College in San Marcos, Texas. To help pay for school, he borrowed $75 from the Johnson City bank. Johnson also had part-time jobs. He worked as a janitor, a secretary to the college president, and a door-to-door salesman.

    Still, Johnson could not meet his expenses. So, he left school to earn some money. Johnson got a job as a teacher and principal. He worked at Welhausen School in Cotulla, Texas.

    After a year, Johnson returned to college. He graduated in 1930. Soon, he went to Houston, Texas. There, Johnson taught public speaking and **debate** at Sam Houston High School.

    Johnson also began helping with Texan Richard M. Kleberg's election campaign. Kleberg won election to the U.S. House of Representatives. He then offered Johnson a job. Johnson moved to Washington, D.C., in 1931. There, he worked as Kleberg's legislative assistant for the next four years.

In 1934, Johnson briefly attended Georgetown University Law School in Washington, D.C. The same year, he met Claudia Alta "Lady Bird" Taylor.

The two quickly fell in love. They married within two months, on November 17. The Johnsons had two daughters. Lynda Bird was born in 1944. Luci Baines followed in 1947.

Mrs. Johnson bought an Austin, Texas, radio station called KTBC in 1943. Later, it was renamed KLBJ. Mrs. Johnson was a smart businesswoman, and the Johnsons became wealthy.

Lynda (lower left) *and Luci* (upper left) *both married while their father was president.*

YOUNG POLITICIAN

In 1935, Johnson became director of the National Youth Administration in Texas. At 26, he was the organization's youngest state director.

Johnson's program gave jobs to students. That way, they could afford to stay in school. It also provided jobs for young people who were not in school. These included **public works** jobs such as building parks, playgrounds, and schools.

In 1937, Johnson was elected to the U.S. House of Representatives. There, he worked to bring electricity to Texans in rural areas. Johnson supported projects for public housing and giving loans to farmers. He also backed soil **conservation** and flood control.

Johnson was a member of the House Naval Affairs Committee. He strongly supported preparing the navy in case of war. Johnson helped plan air training, shipbuilding, and other naval sites in Texas.

On December 7, 1941, Japanese forces attacked the U.S. naval base at Pearl Harbor, Hawaii. The United States then entered **World War II**.

During World War II, Johnson served in the Pacific.

    Johnson became the first congressman to serve on active duty in the war. For his bravery during the war, he received the Silver Star Medal. In 1942, President Franklin D. Roosevelt ordered all congressmen serving in the war back to Washington, D.C. Johnson returned to the House in July.

Johnson first ran for the U.S. Senate in 1941. That year, he lost by just 1,311 votes! He went on to win in 1948, 1954, and 1960.

In 1947, Representative Johnson supported the Taft-Hartley Act. This law protected the rights of workers to organize in unions. It also banned the hiring of only union members. And, it regulated strikes that would cause national emergencies.

Johnson served 12 years in the U.S. House of Representatives. Then in 1948, he ran for the U.S. Senate. Johnson won! There, he served an additional 12 years.

Johnson soon became a **Democratic** Party leader. In 1951, he was elected Democratic **whip**. Two years later, he became Senate **minority leader**. Then in 1955, he became the youngest **majority leader** in Senate history.

On July 2, 1955, Johnson suffered a heart attack. He recovered and returned to the Senate in December. In 1957 and 1960, Johnson helped pass two **civil rights** bills. Both bills concerned voting rights. They were the first civil rights bills passed in more than 80 years.

In 1958, Johnson helped pass the National Aeronautics and Space Act. This formed the National Aeronautics and Space Administration (NASA). Johnson continued his work in the Senate for the next two years.

VICE PRESIDENT JOHNSON

In 1960, Johnson campaigned for the **Democratic** presidential nomination. But the Democrats decided John F. Kennedy should run for president instead. They chose Johnson as Kennedy's **running mate**. The **Republican** Party nominated Richard Nixon for president. Henry Cabot Lodge Jr. was his running mate.

Together, Kennedy and Johnson made a good team. Kennedy was from the North, while Johnson was from the South. As a result, both northerners and southerners voted for them.

Kennedy and Johnson won the election. At the same time, Johnson was reelected to the Senate. In January 1961, he took the Senate oath of office. He immediately resigned. Johnson then took the oath of office to become vice president.

Johnson was an active vice president. He attended **cabinet**, National Security Council, and other White House meetings. Johnson was chairman of the National Aeronautics and Space Council. He was also chairman of the President's Committee on

Equal Employment Opportunity. This group focused on ending racial **discrimination** when hiring workers.

As vice president, Johnson was also in charge of the National Advisory Council for the Peace Corps. The Peace Corps is an organization of American volunteers. They assist people in developing countries with agriculture, health, and education.

The Democrats nominated Kennedy for president on July 13, 1960, in Los Angeles, California. Johnson was nominated for vice president the following day.

Mrs. Johnson (left) *and Mrs. Kennedy* (right) *stood by Johnson's side as he took the oath of office.*

In 1963, Kennedy, Johnson, and their wives traveled to Texas. It was partly to begin working toward the upcoming 1964 election.

On November 22, Kennedy and Johnson rode through downtown Dallas. Kennedy was in the backseat of one car. Johnson was two cars behind him. Suddenly, gunshots rang out. President Kennedy was hit.

When the shots were fired, a **Secret Service** agent pushed Johnson down. He lay over the vice president until they were safe. Kennedy was later pronounced dead at the hospital. Johnson then boarded Air Force One to return to Washington, D.C.

On the airplane, Johnson was sworn in as the thirty-sixth U.S. president. His friend Sarah T. Hughes administered the oath of office. She was a judge from Dallas.

Lee Harvey Oswald was accused of the **assassination**. However, the 24 year old never made it to court. On November 24, local businessman Jack Ruby killed him.

Lee Harvey Oswald

PRESIDENT JOHNSON

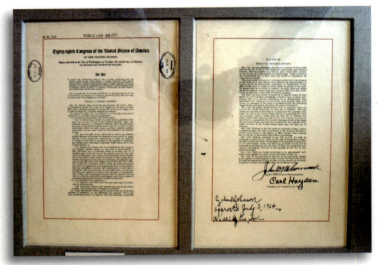

The Civil Rights Act of 1964

In the weeks following Kennedy's death, Johnson showed strong leadership. He helped calm the nation. President Johnson also worked with Congress to pass important laws.

On July 2, 1964, President Johnson signed the historic **Civil Rights** Act. It banned **discrimination** in public places. And, it guaranteed equal voting rights. The act also pushed for the **desegregation** of schools. It allowed the government to hold back money from schools that practiced discrimination.

Johnson worked on laws that would help the poor and support education. He also signed a large tax cut. By now, most of Kennedy's policies had passed. Johnson began working on his own programs.

President Johnson signing the Civil Rights Act of 1964

Meanwhile, there was trouble in Asia. Back in 1954, Vietnam had been divided in two. North Vietnam was Communist. South Vietnam was not.

Elections were planned for 1956 to reunite the countries. But South Vietnam's leader, Ngo Dinh Diem, had refused to participate. The United States had supported his decision.

However, North Vietnam had then attacked South Vietnam. America supported South Vietnam. President Dwight D. Eisenhower and President Kennedy had each helped. They had sent money and military advisers.

Then on August 2 and 4, 1964, North Vietnamese ships attacked two American destroyers. The attack occurred off the coast of North Vietnam in the Gulf of Tonkin. Now, the United States became more involved in the conflict. It became known as the **Vietnam War**.

On August 7, Congress passed the Gulf of Tonkin Resolution. It gave President Johnson the power to prevent and defend against attacks by North Vietnam. This allowed the United States to enter the conflict without officially declaring war. Johnson quickly began sending more American troops to fight.

SUPREME COURT APPOINTMENTS

ABE FORTAS - 1965
THURGOOD MARSHALL - 1967

22

Johnson visited South Vietnam in 1961 while vice president. In 1966, he traveled there again as president.

THE GREAT SOCIETY

In November 1964, Johnson was elected president. At the time, he won the greatest presidential election victory in U.S. history. He earned 61 percent of the **popular vote**.

Johnson's **running mate** was Minnesota senator Hubert H. Humphrey. They defeated **Republican** candidate Barry M. Goldwater. His running mate was William E. Miller.

On January 20, 1965, Johnson was **inaugurated**

Hubert H. Humphrey ran for president in 1968. However, he lost to Richard Nixon.

for his first full term. The previous spring, Johnson had proposed "an end to poverty and racial injustice." He called his plans the Great Society. At his inauguration, Johnson repeated his ideas.

Johnson's Great Society included several programs. Medicare and Medicaid provided health care for the elderly and the poor. Head Start helped poor children get ready for school. Job Corps provided job training and other support for youths.

Thurgood Marshall fought for civil rights throughout his career.

President Johnson also continued to support **civil rights**. In 1965, he signed the Voting Rights Act. This act further protected African-American voting rights.

In January 1966, Johnson appointed the first African-American head of a **cabinet** department. Robert C. Weaver became secretary of the Department of Housing and Urban Development. In 1967, Johnson appointed the first African-American **Supreme Court justice**, Thurgood Marshall.

In Johnson's televised announcement, he said, "I shall not seek, and I will not accept, the nomination of my party for another term as your president."

At the same time, the **Vietnam War** was going badly. Even with America's help, South Vietnam was struggling. North Vietnam had help from China, another Communist country. Also, many South Vietnamese soldiers were trained by and favored North Vietnam. They used **guerrilla warfare** to fight American and other South Vietnamese forces.

President Johnson sent more and more troops to help South Vietnam. At the end of 1967, nearly 500 American soldiers were dying each week. By 1968, about 550,000 American soldiers were in the country. At home, Americans protested the war. Johnson's popularity fell quickly.

By early 1968, many Americans believed the war could not end soon. On March 31, Johnson surprised the nation with three announcements. He spoke on television.

Johnson announced a reduction in the bombing of North Vietnam. And, he proposed the opening of peace talks. President Johnson also stated that he would not run for reelection.

PRESIDENT JOHNSON'S CABINET

FIRST TERM
NOVEMBER 22, 1963– JANUARY 20, 1965

- **STATE –** Dean Rusk
- **TREASURY –** C. Douglas Dillon
- **DEFENSE –** Robert S. McNamara
- **ATTORNEY GENERAL –** Robert F. Kennedy
- **INTERIOR –** Stewart L. Udall
- **AGRICULTURE –** Orville L. Freeman
- **COMMERCE –** Luther H. Hodges
- **LABOR –** W. Willard Wirtz
- **HEALTH, EDUCATION, AND WELFARE –**
  Anthony J. Celebrezze

SECOND TERM
JANUARY 20, 1965– JANUARY 20, 1969

- **STATE –** Dean Rusk
- **TREASURY –** C. Douglas Dillon
  Henry H. Fowler (from April 1, 1965)
  Joseph W. Barr (from December 23, 1968)
- **DEFENSE –** Robert S. McNamara
  Clark M. Clifford (from March 1, 1968)
- **ATTORNEY GENERAL –** Nicholas deBelleville Katzenbach
  Ramsey Clark (from March 10, 1967)
- **INTERIOR –** Stewart L. Udall
- **AGRICULTURE –** Orville L. Freeman
- **COMMERCE –** John T. Connor
  Alexander B. Trowbridge (from June 14, 1967)
  C.R. Smith (from March 6, 1968)
- **LABOR –** W. Willard Wirtz
- **HEALTH, EDUCATION, AND WELFARE –**
  Anthony J. Celebrezze
  John William Gardner (from August 18, 1965)
  Wilbur J. Cohen (from May 9, 1968)
- **HOUSING AND URBAN DEVELOPMENT –**
  Robert C. Weaver (from January 18, 1966)
  Robert Coldwell Wood (from January 7, 1969)
- **TRANSPORTATION –**
  Alan S. Boyd (from January 16, 1967)

BACK AT THE RANCH

January 20, 1969, was Johnson's last day as president. The Johnsons then retired to the LBJ Ranch near Johnson City.

Johnson wrote a book about his time as president. *The Vantage Point: Perspectives of the Presidency, 1963–1969* was published in

Johnson wanted the Lyndon Baines Johnson Library and Museum to help visitors better understand the presidency.

1971. That year, the Lyndon Baines Johnson Library and Museum was **dedicated**. It is on the campus of the University of Texas at Austin.

On January 22, 1973, Lyndon B. Johnson died of a heart attack. Just a few days later, those still fighting agreed to end the **Vietnam War**.

As president, Johnson showed strong leadership after Kennedy's **assassination**. He signed important **civil rights** acts. And, he

started vital social programs. He is also remembered for his part in the **Vietnam War**. Johnson was a congressman, a senator, and a president. In every office, Lyndon B. Johnson worked hard to serve his country.

OFFICE OF THE PRESIDENT

BRANCHES OF GOVERNMENT

The U.S. government is divided into three branches. They are the executive, legislative, and judicial branches. This division is called a separation of powers. Each branch has some power over the others. This is called a system of checks and balances.

EXECUTIVE BRANCH

The executive branch enforces laws. It is made up of the president, the vice president, and the president's cabinet. The president represents the United States around the world. He or she oversees relations with other countries and signs treaties. The president signs bills into law and appoints officials and federal judges. He or she also leads the military and manages government workers.

LEGISLATIVE BRANCH

The legislative branch makes laws, maintains the military, and regulates trade. It also has the power to declare war. This branch consists of the Senate and the House of Representatives. Together, these two houses make up Congress. Each state has two senators. A state's population determines the number of representatives it has.

JUDICIAL BRANCH

The judicial branch interprets laws. It consists of district courts, courts of appeals, and the Supreme Court. District courts try cases. If a person disagrees with a trial's outcome, he or she may appeal. If the courts of appeals support the ruling, a person may appeal to the Supreme Court. The Supreme Court also makes sure that laws follow the U.S. Constitution.

QUALIFICATIONS FOR OFFICE

To be president, a person must meet three requirements. A candidate must be at least 35 years old and a natural-born U.S. citizen. He or she must also have lived in the United States for at least 14 years.

ELECTORAL COLLEGE

The U.S. presidential election is an indirect election. Voters from each state choose electors to represent them in the Electoral College. The number of electors from each state is based on population. Each elector has one electoral vote. Electors are pledged to cast their vote for the candidate who receives the highest number of popular votes in their state. A candidate must receive the majority of Electoral College votes to win.

TERM OF OFFICE

Each president may be elected to two four-year terms. Sometimes, a president may only be elected once. This happens if he or she served more than two years of the previous president's term.

The presidential election is held on the Tuesday after the first Monday in November. The president is sworn in on January 20 of the following year. At that time, he or she takes the oath of office:

I do solemnly swear (or affirm) that I will faithfully execute the office of President of the United States, and will to the best of my ability, preserve, protect and defend the Constitution of the United States.

Line of Succession

The Presidential Succession Act of 1947 defines who becomes president if the president cannot serve. The vice president is first in the line of succession. Next are the Speaker of the House and the President Pro Tempore of the Senate. If none of these individuals is able to serve, the office falls to the president's cabinet members. They would take office in the order in which each department was created:

Secretary of State

Secretary of the Treasury

Secretary of Defense

Attorney General

Secretary of the Interior

Secretary of Agriculture

Secretary of Commerce

Secretary of Labor

Secretary of Health and Human Services

Secretary of Housing and Urban Development

Secretary of Transportation

Secretary of Energy

Secretary of Education

Secretary of Veterans Affairs

Secretary of Homeland Security

Benefits

• While in office, the president receives a salary of $400,000 each year. He or she lives in the White House and has 24-hour Secret Service protection.

• The president may travel on a Boeing 747 jet called Air Force One. The airplane can accommodate 70 passengers. It has kitchens, a dining room, sleeping areas, and a conference room. It also has fully equipped offices with the latest communications systems. Air Force One can fly halfway around the world before needing to refuel. It can even refuel in flight!

• If the president wishes to travel by car, he or she uses Cadillac One. Cadillac One is a Cadillac Deville. It has been modified with heavy armor and communications systems. The president takes Cadillac One along when visiting other countries if secure transportation will be needed.

• The president also travels on a helicopter called Marine One. Like the presidential car, Marine One accompanies the president when traveling abroad if necessary.

• Sometimes, the president needs to get away and relax with family and friends. Camp David is the official presidential retreat. It is located in the cool, wooded mountains in Maryland. The U.S. Navy maintains the retreat, and the U.S. Marine Corps keeps it secure. The camp offers swimming, tennis, golf, and hiking.

• When the president leaves office, he or she receives Secret Service protection for ten more years. He or she also receives a yearly pension of $191,300 and funding for office space, supplies, and staff.

PRESIDENTS AND THEIR TERMS

PRESIDENT	PARTY	TOOK OFFICE	LEFT OFFICE	TERMS SERVED	VICE PRESIDENT
George Washington	None	April 30, 1789	March 4, 1797	Two	John Adams
John Adams	Federalist	March 4, 1797	March 4, 1801	One	Thomas Jefferson
Thomas Jefferson	Democratic-Republican	March 4, 1801	March 4, 1809	Two	Aaron Burr, George Clinton
James Madison	Democratic-Republican	March 4, 1809	March 4, 1817	Two	George Clinton, Elbridge Gerry
James Monroe	Democratic-Republican	March 4, 1817	March 4, 1825	Two	Daniel D. Tompkins
John Quincy Adams	Democratic-Republican	March 4, 1825	March 4, 1829	One	John C. Calhoun
Andrew Jackson	Democrat	March 4, 1829	March 4, 1837	Two	John C. Calhoun, Martin Van Buren
Martin Van Buren	Democrat	March 4, 1837	March 4, 1841	One	Richard M. Johnson
William H. Harrison	Whig	March 4, 1841	April 4, 1841	Died During First Term	John Tyler
John Tyler	Whig	April 6, 1841	March 4, 1845	Completed Harrison's Term	Office Vacant
James K. Polk	Democrat	March 4, 1845	March 4, 1849	One	George M. Dallas
Zachary Taylor	Whig	March 5, 1849	July 9, 1850	Died During First Term	Millard Fillmore

PRESIDENT	PARTY	TOOK OFFICE	LEFT OFFICE	TERMS SERVED	VICE PRESIDENT
Millard Fillmore	Whig	July 10, 1850	March 4, 1853	Completed Taylor's Term	Office Vacant
Franklin Pierce	Democrat	March 4, 1853	March 4, 1857	One	William R.D. King
James Buchanan	Democrat	March 4, 1857	March 4, 1861	One	John C. Breckinridge
Abraham Lincoln	Republican	March 4, 1861	April 15, 1865	Served One Term, Died During Second Term	Hannibal Hamlin, Andrew Johnson
Andrew Johnson	Democrat	April 15, 1865	March 4, 1869	Completed Lincoln's Second Term	Office Vacant
Ulysses S. Grant	Republican	March 4, 1869	March 4, 1877	Two	Schuyler Colfax, Henry Wilson
Rutherford B. Hayes	Republican	March 3, 1877	March 4, 1881	One	William A. Wheeler
James A. Garfield	Republican	March 4, 1881	September 19, 1881	Died During First Term	Chester Arthur
Chester Arthur	Republican	September 20, 1881	March 4, 1885	Completed Garfield's Term	Office Vacant
Grover Cleveland	Democrat	March 4, 1885	March 4, 1889	One	Thomas A. Hendricks
Benjamin Harrison	Republican	March 4, 1889	March 4, 1893	One	Levi P. Morton
Grover Cleveland	Democrat	March 4, 1893	March 4, 1897	One	Adlai E. Stevenson
William McKinley	Republican	March 4, 1897	September 14, 1901	Served One Term, Died During Second Term	Garret A. Hobart, Theodore Roosevelt

PRESIDENTS 13–25, 1850–1901

PRESIDENT	PARTY	TOOK OFFICE	LEFT OFFICE	TERMS SERVED	VICE PRESIDENT
Theodore Roosevelt	Republican	September 14, 1901	March 4, 1909	Completed McKinley's Second Term, Served One Term	Office Vacant, Charles Fairbanks
William Taft	Republican	March 4, 1909	March 4, 1913	One	James S. Sherman
Woodrow Wilson	Democrat	March 4, 1913	March 4, 1921	Two	Thomas R. Marshall
Warren G. Harding	Republican	March 4, 1921	August 2, 1923	Died During First Term	Calvin Coolidge
Calvin Coolidge	Republican	August 3, 1923	March 4, 1929	Completed Harding's Term, Served One Term	Office Vacant, Charles Dawes
Herbert Hoover	Republican	March 4, 1929	March 4, 1933	One	Charles Curtis
Franklin D. Roosevelt	Democrat	March 4, 1933	April 12, 1945	Served Three Terms, Died During Fourth Term	John Nance Garner, Henry A. Wallace, Harry S. Truman
Harry S. Truman	Democrat	April 12, 1945	January 20, 1953	Completed Roosevelt's Fourth Term, Served One Term	Office Vacant, Alben Barkley
Dwight D. Eisenhower	Republican	January 20, 1953	January 20, 1961	Two	Richard Nixon
John F. Kennedy	Democrat	January 20, 1961	November 22, 1963	Died During First Term	Lyndon B. Johnson
Lyndon B. Johnson	Democrat	November 22, 1963	January 20, 1969	Completed Kennedy's Term, Served One Term	Office Vacant, Hubert H. Humphrey
Richard Nixon	Republican	January 20, 1969	August 9, 1974	Completed First Term, Resigned During Second Term	Spiro T. Agnew, Gerald Ford

PRESIDENTS 26–37, 1901–1974

PRESIDENT	PARTY	TOOK OFFICE	LEFT OFFICE	TERMS SERVED	VICE PRESIDENT
Gerald Ford	Republican	August 9, 1974	January 20, 1977	Completed Nixon's Second Term	Nelson A. Rockefeller
Jimmy Carter	Democrat	January 20, 1977	January 20, 1981	One	Walter Mondale
Ronald Reagan	Republican	January 20, 1981	January 20, 1989	Two	George H.W. Bush
George H.W. Bush	Republican	January 20, 1989	January 20, 1993	One	Dan Quayle
Bill Clinton	Democrat	January 20, 1993	January 20, 2001	Two	Al Gore
George W. Bush	Republican	January 20, 2001	January 20, 2009	Two	Dick Cheney
Barack Obama	Democrat	January 20, 2009			Joe Biden

"A President's hardest task is not to do what is right, but to know what is right." Lyndon B. Johnson

WRITE TO THE PRESIDENT

You may write to the president at:

The White House
1600 Pennsylvania Avenue NW
Washington, DC 20500

You may e-mail the president at:

comments@whitehouse.gov

GLOSSARY

assassinate - to murder a very important person, usually for political reasons.

cabinet - a group of advisers chosen by the president to lead government departments.

civil rights - the individual rights of a citizen, such as the right to vote or freedom of speech.

conservation - the planned management of natural resources to protect them from damage or destruction.

debate - a contest in which two sides argue for or against something.

dedicate - to open to public use.

Democrat - a member of the Democratic political party. Democrats believe in social change and strong government.

desegregation (dee-seh-grih-GAY-shuhn) - the elimination of the separation of people based on race.

discrimination (dihs-krih-muh-NAY-shuhn) - unfair treatment based on factors such as a person's race, religion, or gender.

guerrilla warfare (guh-RIH-luh WAWR-fehr) - a form of war based on making surprise attacks behind enemy lines.

inauguration (ih-naw-gyuh-RAY-shuhn) - a ceremony in which a person is sworn into office.

justice - a judge on the U.S. Supreme Court.

majority leader - the leader of the party that has the greatest number of votes in a legislative body, such as the U.S. Senate.

minority leader - the leader of a party that does not have the greatest number of votes in a legislative body, such as the U.S. Senate.

popular vote - the vote of the entire body of people with the right to vote.

public works - projects the government pays for, such as roads, dams, or sewers.

Republican - a member of the Republican political party. Republicans are conservative and believe in small government.

running mate - a candidate running for a lower-rank position on an election ticket, especially the candidate for vice president.

Secret Service - a federal law enforcement agency. Its duties include conducting criminal investigations and protecting national leaders, such as the president, and visiting foreign leaders.

Supreme Court - the highest, most powerful court in the United States.

Vietnam War - from 1957 to 1975. A long, failed attempt by the United States to stop North Vietnam from taking over South Vietnam.

whip - a member of a political party who is in charge of making sure party members attend important voting sessions.

World War II - from 1939 to 1945, fought in Europe, Asia, and Africa. Great Britain, France, the United States, the Soviet Union, and their allies were on one side. Germany, Italy, Japan, and their allies were on the other side.

WEB SITES

To learn more about Lyndon B. Johnson, visit ABDO Publishing Company on the World Wide Web at **www.abdopublishing.com**. Web sites about Lyndon B. Johnson are featured on our Book Links page. These links are routinely monitored and updated to provide the most current information available.

INDEX